The GREAT LOVER'S Manifesto

DAVE GRANT

HARVEST HOUSE PUBLISHERS
Eugene, Oregon 97402

Other books by Dave Grant

The Ultimate Power (Revell)
Compass For Conscience (Revell)
Heavy Questions (Regal)
You've Got What It Takes (Rainbow)
Would You Believe (Regal)

The GREAT
LOVERS
Manifesto

Copyright © 1986 by Harvest House Publishers
Eugene, Oregon 97402

Library of Congress Catalog Card Number 85-060124
ISBN 0-89081-481-3

Printed in the United States of America.

First edition

To Simone

Contents

"He who serves

God from love

devotes himself to His law and
to the observance of
His Commandments, and
walks in the path of wisdom,
    not because of any
    worldly advantage,
    nor to protect himself
    from evil,
    nor to inherit good
    thereafter,
He does the right
because it is right,
    though in the end
    the blessing will not
    fail him."

Moses Maimonides, 1135-1204

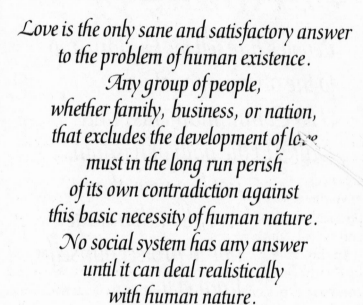

Love is the only sane and satisfactory answer
to the problem of human existence.
Any group of people,
whether family, business, or nation,
that excludes the development of love
must in the long run perish
of its own contradiction against
this basic necessity of human nature.
No social system has any answer
until it can deal realistically
with human nature.

The Meaning of Love

*I*f we understand the nature of love, we will see its general absence today and understand the social conditions which are the result of its absence.

Without love we lose the will to live. Our mental and physical vitality is impaired, our resistance is lowered, and we succumb to illness.

In this book we are considering self-sacrificial "agape" love rather than the sensual attraction of "eros" or the common experience called friendship. Self-sacrificial love has a profound effect on all our relationships, whether man / woman, parent / child, friend / friend, teacher / student, or management / labor. This kind of love touches the core of our human nature.

The better you love—
> *The better you live,*
> *The better you parent,*
> *The better you husband,*
> *The better you manage,*
> *The better you teach,*
> *The better you sell.*

When is the best time in life to speak authoritatively about love? When you are being put to the test! As we commit ourselves to growth and spiritual development, the testing and trials do not get less — they become sterner. The commitment to love does not make life easier — but it does make it better. The secret to living is not to be void of problems and challenges. The secret is to have the resources to face each day.

If I have love in my life,
it can make up for many things I lack.
If I do not have love in my life,
no matter what else there is,
it is not enough.

Each of us can experience the best life has to offer in a quiet and powerful way. The quiet revolution has begun. Love is the only guarantee of return on the investment of *our words, our goods,* and *our lives.*

Heavenly Father,
I praise and thank You for this new
day. I thank You for all Your goodness
and faithfulness throughout my life. You
have granted me many blessings; let me
also accept tribulation from Your hand.
You will not lay on me more than I can
bear, for You make things work together
for good for Your children.

Love Is an Effort

A number of bees were taken along on a flight into space in order to see how they would handle the experience of weightlessness. In the weightless atmosphere they were able to float in space without any effort. The report on the experiment was summed up in these words:
"They enjoyed the ride, but they died."

*W*ithout effort we atrophy. We need tension in order to stretch and grow because we are basically lazy. We really want the easy way: We look for shortcuts; we really believe we can get something for nothing.

But we're not going to grow until we are willing to admit that life is a struggle, and that the struggle is good because it keeps us alive.

We seldom drift into anything worthwhile. I don't know of anything in my life that gets better with neglect. My garden and yard certainly don't. My automobile doesn't. My body doesn't. My marriage doesn't. These all need constant attention and maintenance. And, if I *value* them, that is exactly what they get.

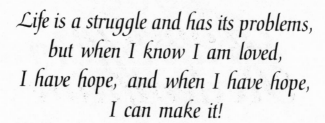

Life is a struggle and has its problems,
but when I know I am loved,
I have hope, and when I have hope,
I can make it!

Love is not
what makes the world go 'round;
it's what makes the ride worthwhile.

A true lover knows,
like the marvelous bee,
that effort will bring us hope
and ultimate growth.
We are kept alive by doing
what we were meant to do.

Love Is Redemptive

Redemptive love—
> Covers the wrong
> Takes the pain
> Takes the blame
> Takes the punishment
> Takes the consequences.

*T*o what extent am I willing to bear the pain to cover someone else's pain...joyfully?

Love covers a multitude of sins (1 Peter 4:8). Love covers in order for healing to take place.

Love does not gossip or slander or repeat rumor. Love gets *under* and supports. Love bears and carries a marriage when passion has faded into dreary toleration. It holds onto the possibility of a miracle of re-creation, of rekindling.

A true lover speaks only with good purpose.

Faults grow thin when love grows thick. Love believes the best.

In a weekly news magazine, a columnist reviewed the books written by a woman of international reputation and concluded that she was a "deeply flawed human being."

In a subsequent issue was the following letter to the editor:

> Those who knew and loved her will have a far different impression. She lived in our home for the last years of her life and was a very real "second mother" to me. She had a harsh temper and was at times impatient and tended to sometimes jump to conclusions without sufficient data, but these were ordinary flaws. I saw her as a loving parent, as a good and often brilliant teacher and as a generous benefactor. It is a pity that these aspects of her life are virtually ignored in your review.

Redemption is involvement,
*   not isolation.*
Redemption is caring,
*   not passing by on the other side.*

Our relationship with each other on the horizontal is similar to that with God on the vertical.

If anyone says he L
                           O
                           V
                           E
                           S

                           G
                           O
                           D
                           but HATES HIS BROTHER
he is a liar.

> *When I was hungry,*
>> *you gave me food;*
>
> *when thirsty,*
>> *you gave me a drink;*
>
> *when a stranger,*
>> *you took me into your home.*
>
> *When I was ill,*
>> *you came to my help;*
>
> *when I was naked,*
>> *you clothed me;*
>
> *when in prison,*
>> *you visited me.*

Anything you did for one of my brothers, however humble, you did for me (Matthew 25:35-40).

Love is involved.
Love is redemptive.

Love Loves the Unlovely

When we accept *all* of a person, it does not mean that we accept everything he does, but that we will not reject all of him for the parts we do not accept.

Unless society is knit together with love, there is only efficient organization; and when efficiency is the highest value, persons are transformed into things whose value is their contribution to making things run. Without true love, efficiency can excuse everything. The weak, the voiceless, the unborn may all be sacrificed at the altar of efficiency.

A true lover loves the unlovely.

Love accepts because it loves. Love does not accept a person because of something on the part of that person. Love does not require the object of its love to be lovable. Love just loves.

Love does not put the responsibility of being loved on the other person.

Love's irony is that
when I need love the most
I am the most unlovely.
Compassion for "nice" people
is not compassion.
Compassion for the unlovely
is compassion.

Love Believes the Best

*L*ove looks for the best in people. Love would rather believe the best and occasionally be disappointed than believe the worst and never be disappointed.

Love does not react to symptoms of behavior, but responds to need. Love gives you the benefit of the doubt. Love, looking through the eyes of faith, sees you for what you can be, while accepting you as you are.

Love is the power to believe that every person is of infinite worth in relationship to God, is redeemable, and can become good.

Love does not fail to recognize wrong, or pretend it doesn't matter, but love does have a transformed *response* to wrong, to faults and blemishes which may appear in other people. Love looks beyond the *fault* and sees the *need*.

Love has the faith to see what a person would be like if he were free, radiant, loving, and happy.

> *"If I treat you as you are,*
> *you will remain as you are.*
> *If I treat you as if you were*
> *what you could be, that is what*
> *you will become"* (Goethe).

Through the eyes of love you see her as alert rather than nosy, thrifty rather than stingy, expressive rather than too talkative, sensitive rather than touchy, confident rather than cocky.

A true lover believes the best about every person and every circumstance.

Love Doesn't Fear Losing

Thinking of your life as stewardship—that you are not your own—means that you have no fear of failure.

Love's submissive authority wins because it doesn't fear losing.

Rebellion's tyrannical slavery loses by fearing defeat. Love's submission is triumphant assurance.

Rebellion is competitive struggle. Love's submission is a grace-filled being.

Rebellion is exhausting effort. Love's submission is peaceful obedience.

Rebellion is strife, war, a "win-lose" situation.

There is no success without sacrifice. There is no crown without a cross. The refusal to pay the price that success demands is the number one reason for failure.

Self-denial is the daring commitment of
>   your name
>   your reputation
>   your integrity
>   your ego
>   on the altar of God's call to serve.

Positive self-denial is denying your ego the selfish protection from a possible humiliating failure that might occur if you tried to carry out God's plan.

The more lovingly we live our lives, the more *risks* we take. The greatest risk is: Growing up, being mature, being responsible, being accountable . . . all of which is love.

Love Bears All Things

*L*ove drives us to do things for people that they cannot do for themselves, and to *not do* for them what they *can*.

Love's goal for others is growth toward maturity. Love holds people accountable. Love knows that we learn by doing, that doing requires choices, that choices require responsiblity.

You cannot be mature and irresponsible.
You cannot be loving and negative,
or positive and fearful.
Making decisions requires choices.
Choice involves options.
Options demand priorities.
Priorities reveal values.
Values determine motivation.
Motivation equals morality.

Love bears all the weaknesses, errors, and pettiness of children. Love allows an eight-year-old to be an eight-year-old.

Love is willing to go out of its way to reduce people's burdens by willingly and joyously sharing their sorrows and hardships.

Love seeks to break down barriers between people and not build its own.

Love's wisdom knows when to share another person's burdens. Love is not eager to say, "You made your bed, now you must lie in it."

A true lover is willing to bear all things in a responsible way.

Love quietly bears another person's burdens without fanfare or a sense of interference.

Love feels and bears the grief of a neighbor's lost child. Love feels and suffers the pangs of a neighbor's hunger.

When a friend does wrong, love comes alongside to help bear the guilt.

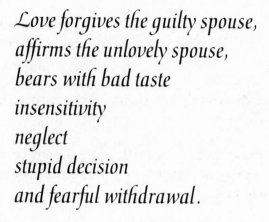

Love forgives the guilty spouse,
affirms the unlovely spouse,
bears with bad taste
insensitivity
neglect
stupid decision
and fearful withdrawal.

Love Shares

There is no limit to what a person can do if he doesn't care who gets the credit. One of the major fears of management is delegation. Delegation is passing on responsibility and authority. Delegation is training other people to do the job and then letting them run with it. The attitude "If I don't do it, it won't be done right" is a jealous, fear-filled attitude that keeps people stunted. The real issue may be "If I don't do it, it won't be done my way." Love's power allows someone else's way to be different without being wrong.

People respond in three ways to ownership:
What's mine is mine
(immature and fearful).
What's yours is mine
(selfish and fearful).
What's mine I share with you
(plentiful and loving).

In parenting, the main objective is similar to that of management: to bring those for whom you are initially responsible to a full position of personal responsibility and authority for their own life. In other words, "to put yourself out of business." In basic terms it is the power of sharing responsibility.

When the relationship begins at birth, the parent is 100 percent responsible for the child's well-being and the child 0 percent. The objective over the next 16 to 21 years is to completely turn the percentages around. The ultimate goal is for the child to arrive at 100 percent and the parent to be at 0 percent. A parent has succeeded when the child reaches maturity and is able to basically function on his own in interdependent relationships.

With this opportunity to make his own decisions goes the responsibility of those decisions.

When parents and managers begin to see what their primary function is, they will not be threatened when they share and delegate responsibility.

Love Is Surrender

Many of us are afraid of being needy. Our experience has been that people tend to take advantage of us or manipulate us when we are needy.

In business, an obvious example of this is the theory of supply and demand. When there is tremendous demand and very little supply, the common practice is to raise the price... to take advantage of people in their neediness.

After I have experienced the hurt and pain of being needy, I determine that the only way I can keep this from happening to me again is to be self-sufficient and protective of myself. When I am self-sufficient and don't need anyone, I don't care about the rest of the world. When I need you, I am at your mercy. When I am a true lover and you are at my mercy, I will love you, not exploit you.

In every relationship we ask the question "If I become needy, will you love me or take advantage of me?" It is difficult for us to admit neediness because we interpret it as weakness. However, the *fear* of neediness is the weakness. When I am no longer afraid of neediness, I am no longer afraid of love.

> *I can only receive love in my neediness,*
> *not in my self-sufficiency.*
> *It is difficult to give something*
> *to someone who has everything.*
> *Self-sufficient people are lonely people.*

The fear of dependence, the unwillingness to surrender a certain portion of my sovereignty or self-sufficiency, to refuse to trust someone else with me — is to choose to be alone.

Love Is Unconditional

Love does not say:
"I love you because you measure up
to my standards and meet my conditions."
Love says:
"I love you for no good reason."

*L*ove is unconditional when nothing is unforgivable. Most of us have something we consider intolerable — something we could never put up with.

Tolerance is not a virtue if you don't believe anything. You can set your standards as high as you want to as long as your forgiveness standard is a step higher.

To ask for pardon (a gift of love) while we do not repent and cease from sin is a gross insult to God.

The receiving of unconditional love is humiliating because I must allow myself to be loved for no reason. I don't have to be lovable to be loved. I am loved because of God's character, not mine. If I am to love you, or anyone else, it will be for the same reason: It is my character, not yours. On what does my lovability depend? Nothing.

On what does my experiencing love depend? My willingness to receive your gift.

You can ask me, "What can I do to be a better wife (or husband, or parent, or child, or friend)," but you can't ask me, "What can I *do* to get you to love me?"

No sooner do we believe that God loves us than we have an impulse to believe that He does so not because of what He is but because of what we are, because we are intrinsically lovable.

The truth is that with God's love there is nothing I need to do in order to be loved. God's love need not be acquired; indeed it *cannot* be acquired. It need not be deserved, nor can it be produced or controlled. It is there as a blessing, and there is nothing I can do to create it.

If we need to deserve love, we always have the feeling that it could disappear. Deserved love easily leaves a bitter feeling that one is not loved for oneself, but that one is loved only because one *pleases* and that in the final analysis one is not loved at all but *used*!

*God's love says, "There is no misdeed
which could deprive you of my love,
of my desire for your happiness."*

Love Is Nonpossessive Delight

*I*t is normal to want what we delight in and to *not* want what we do not delight in.

Love as a nonpossessive delight allows us to pass up our chances to seize or possess what we perceive as "belonging" to us. Love does not seek its own rights.

Love does not need to possess in order to guarantee tomorrow for delight. Love enjoys the moment.

Is it possible that we could begin early in life to teach young people to have a nonpossessive delight in the opposite sex? To do so would be to teach them something about love.

The natural process is to reach the age of puberty and discover the opposite sex. Before long there is a special attraction toward one in whom there is an element of delight. Having discovered something in which we delight, the next step is to "have it," to take it out of circulation, to make it mine, to go steady with it. I will possess this person, using him (her) to meet my ego needs as long as I find him delightful.

But the chances are that I will lose my delight and therefore no longer want to have him, or that someone else will come along in whom I find *more* delight.

Without realizing it, a habit is formed which becomes a real strain on the commitment of marriage. Today's divorce rate reflects this habit. Marriage is not "going steady"; it is going "until death do us part." It has vows about "better or worse, in sickness and health" to sustain those moments when there is no delight.

How much better it would be to start early in life experiencing love as a nonpossessive delight!

It is impossible to delight in or enjoy anything we cling to, because of our fear of losing it.

Love Breaks the Bondage

*L*ove and money and success seem to be neurotically entangled by most people. Many people who are consciously striving for money are subconsciously striving to achieve and obtain love.

Many of the ways thought necessary to make oneself *lovable* are the same as those necessary to make oneself *successful*: good looks, brains, and achievements.

There is an unexpressed fear that if you are dumb, or ugly, or unproductive, you will be neither loved or successful.

There is indeed a relationship between love and money, but it is different from the above.

Most of us have been taught that our heart, (our love), is where our treasure is. Money is not in itself an evil. However, we can have an *attitude* toward money that makes it an evil in our life.

Money becomes a problem when we believe it will solve our problems, that it will meet our needs for independence or security or happiness or love. We "worship" money when we believe it will be our "salvation."

Fearful people think of success in terms of how much they can get and hold onto.

Loving people think of success in terms of how much they can give away.

The significance of the giving is not the *amount* but the *attitude*.

*God will trust us with as much
as we are willing to release.
We are channels, not reservoirs.
We are stewards, not owners.*

*Realizing that he is a steward,
the loving person wisely gives of
his time, his talents, and his energy.*

*Generosity is good deeds that are done
quietly
inconspicuously
and immediately forgotten.*

*No one is too poor to give;
he is too poor <u>not</u> to give.*

*The principle of giving will either
break the <u>spirit of poverty</u> in your life
if you think you are poor,
or it will break your <u>bondage to things</u>
if you are wealthy.*

Love Gives Value

*L*ove affirms and esteems the uniqueness of the one loved. Love makes no comparisons.

We usually value something only as it relates to us:
    something we can use
    something we can enjoy
    something we can benefit from.

It's just an ordinary baseball until Babe Ruth hits it out of the park. It's just another painting until signed by Rembrandt. It's just a piece of glass until the Tiffany stamp is discovered on it.

Rarity creates value. Love gives it high value whether or not I am benefited by it. Love gives eloquent speech value. Love gives understanding and knowledge value. If I give my goods to the poor and my body as a sacrifice, only love will give me a guaranteed return on my investment.

What do I want love to tell me? That—
     I count
     I am valued
     I have a sense of goodness
     I am a precious person
     I am loved
         accepted
         forgiven
         free.

If I have one, <u>I have them</u> all!

Love Is a Constant Challenge

Love is not a resting place.
It is moving, working together, growing.
Whether there is harmony or conflict,
joy or sadness is secondary
to the fundamental fact
that two people experience themselves
from the essence of their existence,
that they are one with each other
by being one with themselves,
rather than fleeing from themselves.

*L*ove is not the absence of conflict. Real conflicts between two people which are experienced on a deep level of reality are not destructive. They lead to clarification, producing a catharsis from which both persons emerge with more knowledge and more strength.

An idle, inactive, inefficient believer is a misnomer. If the *will* is active, the *life* must be. A saint *must* manifest his love or benevolence.

Love is *good-willing*, or the choice of the highest good of God and the universe as a goal. Love is the best possible means to achieve that goal for its own sake, and not to gratify self.

Selfishness is a spirit of self-gratification. Selfish "love" makes the relation of good to myself the condition of choosing it.

Love does not seek its own,
but the good of others.
Love is a challenge because it cares.

Love Is Impartial

Love is no respecter of persons.

Love just loves. It doesn't pick and choose. It recognizes no privileged classes. Love has no favorites, no prejudices.

Love knows neither Jew nor Greek, bond nor free, white nor black. Love accounts all people as people. By virtue of their common humanity it calls every man a brother and seeks the interest of each one.

The fact that a person is a person, and not that he is of our party, or our complexion, or our town or nation—that he is a creature of God, that he is capable of virtue and happiness—these are the considerations of divinely impartial love.

But because our love is limited in time and energy, it must put forth its efforts in the directions where there is the prospect of accomplishing the most good.

More good will result in the world by each of us giving particular attention to the promotion of those interests that are sufficiently within our reach and sufficiently under our influence that we are able to attend to them.

Some interests of great value we may be under no obligation to promote because we have other responsibilities that have a higher priority.

What counts is not the particular persons to whom good can be done, but the amount of good that can be accomplished.

It is not because my family is more valuable in itself than that of my neighbor's family, but because my relations can afford me better opportunity for doing them good, that I am under particular obligation to aim first at promoting their good.

True love is not an impulse from the feelings
and seldom runs with natural inclinations.

Love seeks the welfare of <u>all</u>,
and works no ill to <u>any</u>.

Love seeks opportunity to do good to all people,
especially toward those who are of the
household of the faith.

Love Is Transparent

Love and authenticity are inseparable partners.

Love is an open book.

Love is open arms.

Love needs no second-guessing.

Love doesn't have to be on guard.

Love doesn't have to watch its language.

Love is pure in heart.

Love has no pretenses.

Love is the same on Sunday morning in a religious environment as it is on Monday morning in a secular environment.

A true lover is willing and able to let other people know and love him deeply.

If you are ever at his mercy, you can trust him, can depend on him. Where there is perfect love there is no fear.

A loving person is congruent. Congruence means being a real person.

Love doesn't need to hide behind the mask of self-sufficiency or self-justification.

Love has no need to prove superiority or adequacy. As a rule, we reveal a weakness by what we try to prove.

Love has no need for scapegoating or rationalizing; love is able and willing to acknowledge error or fault. Congruency is transparent; it is consistent.

You can do the kind thing without being loving, but you can't be loving and unkind.

You can be moral and unloving, but you can't be loving and immoral.

You can be religious and unloving, but you can't express your true spiritual nature without sharing love with another.

Love Is Liberating

*Love offers a person roots
(a sense of belonging)
and wings
(a sense of freedom).*

ove does not seek to control for its own satisfaction. Love uses its power to serve other people's needs. Selfishness uses its power to manipulate others to meet its own needs. Love wants the other to be free, to be all he was meant to be for his *own* sake and not mine.

When we deal with people in their inner freedom, we can never be secure. This is not because other people are unreliable, but because when I depend on the freedom of other people, I have no control over them. If they are reliable, it is not because they let me control them or have disposal over them but because they freely choose to be reliable. In that case I have no feeling of security, no sense of control.

Similarly, I have no control over God. He is never at my disposal. No matter how much I believe in God's reliability, that reliability comes out of God's freedom. But because God is love, He is totally reliable.

A mother's love is tested by her willingness to encourage and support her child's release. It requires unselfishness — the ability to give everything and to want nothing but the happiness of the child.

A true lover is respectful, which implies an absence of exploitation. I want the loved person to grow and unfold for his *own* sake and in his *own* ways — not for the purpose of serving me. I love the other person for *who he is* — not because I need him as an object for my use.

Love which wants nothing for itself is the ultimate virtue. Most mothers can love when the child is young, but only the really loving woman who is happier in giving than in taking can release the child when they are older. It is difficult but it is done because it is in the child's best interest and not the parent's.

She can be a truly loving mother *only* if she can love in a larger sense — if she is able to love her husband
        other children
        strangers
        all human beings
        life itself.

Love Enjoys Creation

We can enjoy the things of God's creation enough to enrich our lives while we have them, but not so much that they impoverish our lives when they are gone. Denial of God's creation may be as serious as indulgence. We must offer things neither worship nor contempt.

In God's creation there are two orders:
things and people.
God's intention was that people be loved
and things be used.
Our greatest sin is that we use people
to get the things we love.

Love enjoys everybody's good things. Selfishness is too envious at the good things of others to even enjoy its own.

Love is able to delight in things because it knows that things are *created*, which means they are gifts of the Creator meant to be received.

If I realize that all I have is a gift (talent, beauty, brains, spouse, children, etc.), I can enjoy and delight in what I have received without being possessive.

The end result of my delight and enjoyment is not conceit but gratitude.

Those who need possessions believe that possessions have life-giving power. They believe that with possessions they can control and cope with life.

Possessions give a false sense of security, the false feeling we have whenever we believe we have control or disposal over our own lives.

Possessions free us from having to rely on other people, thereby making relationship impossible.

Love enjoys creation because it doesn't seek security through the possession of creation.

Love Is Courage

*L*ove is the active concern for the life and growth of that which we love.

The essence of love is to labor for something, to make something grow.

Love and labor are inseparable. We love what we labor for, and we labor for what we love.

It is an illusion to believe that we can separate life in such a way that we are productive in the area of love but unproductive in all other areas.

Love is an act of faith, and whoever is of little faith is of little love.

Love is an act of courage.

The goal of love is not to turn us into docile creatures, but to employ our aggressive energies in the creative services of mankind.

Love is an effort. Love is always either work or courage.

The most loving thing I will ever do will probably be hard, not easy, because it will be done with courage, *against* what I feel.

If what I do is not of work or courage, it is not an act of love. There are no exceptions!

Love Initiates

*Love is willing to initiate risk,
going first, reaching out, opening up,
again and again and again.*

When we are consciously afraid of not *being loved*, the real, (though usually unconscious) fear, is that of *loving*.

To love means to commit ourself without guarantee, to give ourself completely in the hope that our love will produce love in the loved person.

How bold we get when we are sure of being loved! Failure doesn't mean a thing when our relationship is secure.

God wants us to live life to the edges, and whether we do it perfectly or imperfectly, we are still loved. So let us live life!

Love does not demand its own way. In traditional marriage a husband has certain rights and a wife has certain rights, but in a truly spiritual marriage this is not true. Neither husband nor wife has any rights: They have only the privilege of loving, only the privilege of sharing, only the privilege of giving, but no right to demand anything of the other.

In love a husband does not have to support a wife. He is free to share without the bondage of being legally compelled to do so.

In love a wife experiences the great joy of giving and sharing spontaneously — an offering of the heart and not the law court. In your hand you hold my heart.

When you know you are loved
you are free to tell the truth
about what you think,
feel
value
love
honor
esteem
hate
fear
desire
hope for
believe in
are committed to—
and this brings growth.

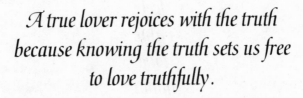

*A true lover rejoices with the truth
because knowing the truth sets us free
to love truthfully.*

Love Rejoices With the Truth

*T*ruth is reality. Whatever is not true is not real. Love never rejoices in evil because evil anywhere, in any form, is antilove.

Love does not rejoice in evil because evil keeps us from true fulfillment, from being all that God meant us to be.

Love is a lover of truth—even about myself. Truth is the reality that sets me free.

That which is false is not real, or loving, or true. Love does not gossip. It does not delight in bad news. It believes the best.

When you receive some bad news regarding someone you love, the response will be, "I don't believe it. It can't be true. Not him."

When you receive the same bad news regarding someone you don't choose to love, the response will be, "I'm not surprised. It figures that he would do something like that."

Love Is Grateful

*L*ove recognizes that every gift and talent comes from God. It boasts of nothing but the goodness of God.

Love recognizes the responsibility to use and develop its gifts, but not with pride, arrogance, or patronizing.

Love does not think more highly of itself that it should.

Love is willing to be known for who I really am — no more and no less. I am what I am by the grace of God.

Because love is grateful, it is never irritable. Love is not irritable because its ego is not at stake. Love is willing to suffer inconvenience so that someone else may turn from a meaningless existence to purposeful living.

Love is grateful because it realizes that all of life is a gift, an act of grace, a mystery.

I am a steward of gifts:
>My marriage is a gift
>My children are a gift
>My talents are a gift
>My friends are a gift.

Being grateful precludes the possibility of conceit. Being grateful for what I am and have is a form of self-acceptance. I am a creature; I have been designed. To be created in the image of God is an awesome responsibility. God the Father from His great heart wants me to succeed. He is for me. He even comes alongside me to share my task, to make my burden lighter.

When I have finished my apprenticeship in life, I want to give back to Him all He has trusted me with and hear Him say, "Well done."

The gift of unconditional love is mine when I
>*claim it*
>*accept it*
>*receive it gratefully*
>>*no questions asked!*

Love Endures All Things

*L*ove is able to endure because of its focus on the "Author and Finisher of my faith."

Jesus endured the cross because of the joy that was to come. Paul said, "I have learned to get along whether I have much or little. I know how to live with nothing or with everything. I have learned to be content whether full or hungry.... I can do everything God asks me to with the help of Christ, who strengthens me."

To endure is the power to hold on!

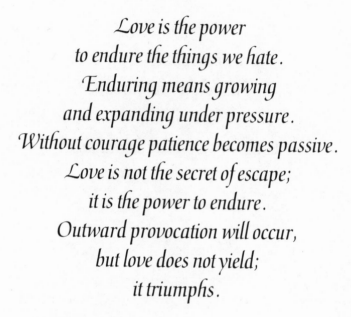

*Love is the power
to endure the things we hate.
Enduring means growing
and expanding under pressure.
Without courage patience becomes passive.
Love is not the secret of escape;
it is the power to endure.
Outward provocation will occur,
but love does not yield;
it triumphs.*

Love appreciates gratitude,
but doesn't require it.
Love is a gift;
it has no hooks or conditions.

Love Is a Gift

*F*or the fearful, giving is thought of as deprivation, as being cheated, as an impoverishment. The fearful are afraid of giving themselves, and hence of loving.

For the true lover, giving is the highest expression of power. In the act of giving I experience my strength, my wealth, my power. I experience myself as overflowing, spending, alive — and joyous. Giving is an expression of my aliveness.

The true lover does not give in order to receive; he gives because giving is in itself exquisite joy!

Because love is a gift, there is no debt. Love doesn't say:

> "After all I did for you!"
> "You owe me one."
> "You didn't appreciate what I did for you."

Love Never Fails

*L*ove never fails because it is the only power in this life that is self-generating.

> *It is the only reality we have in*
> *time*
> *that will go unchanged into*
> *eternity.*
> *Only love is a sure sign of maturity.*
> *Love never fails.*
> *Love enlarges*
> *rather than diminishes*
> *the self.*

*It fills the self rather than
    depleting it.
When love comes in,
    defenses drop,
    fatigue moves out.
Love does not need to prove,
        protect, or
        validate itself.
Love is.*

Love's Truest Measure

The true measure of a loving person can be determined by watching him closely and observing how he treats people who can do him absolutely no good.

Only in the love of those who do not serve a purpose does love begin to unfold.

To love one's own flesh and blood is no great achievement.

In the Old Testament the central object of man's love was to be:
> the poor
> the stranger
> the widow
> the orphan
> the enemy.

Most acts of love will be done unnoticed, because love's generosity is good deeds that are done quietly and inconspicuously, then immediately forgotten.

Love Is Healing

*Love's desire is to heal
and help another person.*

*L*ove is glad when the other is helped even if no one knows or cares that it was he who helped.

If we keep caring for the person even if he forgets completely that he owed us anything at all, we have been with God for that one loving moment.

Sometimes healing requires incising a wound to get rid of the poison. Healing often involves pain.

Healing follows a willingness to risk exposing how wrong I have been.

I have a *choice* to let forgiveness, reconciliation, and healing happen. Or I can refuse to let it happen.

Because loves wants to heal, it doesn't brood over wrong. It doesn't focus on wrong so as to magnify it and justify the feelings of revenge.

Love isn't glad
when other people go wrong.
Love doesn't think:
 "I told you so" or
 "You got what you had coming."
Love is healing. It cannot be glad when
others make a wrong move or an unwise
step that is contrary to God's law and
leads to their downfall.

This must be applied to the person with whom you are competing, your opponent, your enemy. There are no exceptions!

Because love is healing, it is slow to expose; it knows when to be silent. Loving people do not willingly mention or expose the faults or failings of others. To allow healing, love never gossips or passes on a rumor. Love asks:
 Is it true?
 Is it loving?
 Is it necessary?

Love doesn't seek to put the other person in the wrong.

Love's intent is to communicate toward intimacy—not to be right.

Love Is Not a Feeling

The *giving* of love is an act of the will that may or may not include feelings. Anyone humbly *receiving* the gift of genuine love will probably experience some very deep feelings.

But a loving relationship needs the warm and loving feelings to support the intentions of my love. Passion first moves me to make a promise of fidelity, but then the quiet power of true love enables me to keep the promise.

Love has a lot of feelings, but feelings don't always mean real love. If I love you I will probably experience passion, but an experience of passion doesn't mean I love you.

We like or are fond of or have good feelings toward some people and not others. Liking a person makes it easier to be loving, but it is not to be confused with love. Our liking may be simply because it is to our own advantage.

A doting mother may be tempted by natural affection to spoil her child—to gratify her own affectionate impulses at the expense of the child's real happiness later on. Although affection may not be love, true love leads to affection.

The worldly person treats certain people kindly because he "likes" them. The true lover treats everyone kindly and finds himself liking more and more people.

Emotions and feelings are purely an involuntary state of mind. Love consists of a choice, an intention. The conscience must approve this love, this choice, this intention.

Envy, jealousy, ambition, and greed are passions. With passion man is driven by motivations of which he himself may not be aware.

Love is an action, an awareness, the practice of my resources, which can be practiced only in freedom and never as the result of compulsion.

Love Extends Itself

Love is the willingness to extend myself for the purpose of nurturing my own or another person's spiritual growth. Love moves against my natural laziness. Love moves against entropy.

If someone demands that you go one mile, you can go on the defensive and fight back, or you can use your offensive surprise and initiate the loving thing: Extend yourself and give *more* than is asked or expected. "If someone forces you to go a mile, go with him two" (Matthew 5:41).

Love is not defensive; it is the perfect offense to absorb and thereby overcome the wrong.

When parents become angry at the trouble and inconvenience that their child brings into their lives, resenting the extra work he causes them, they lose their valuable perspective on the privilege and responsibility of parenthood. The child becomes a burden and a bother to them. When this happens, they govern the child to reduce their own personal discomforts instead of governing the child primarily for his own welfare.

Love goes the second mile.
Love gives the overcoat with the coat.

Love exists when the satisfaction, security, and development of the other person become as significiant to me as my own satisfaction, security, and development.

Love Wrongs No One

*L*ove does no wrong to anyone. That is why it fully satisfies all of God's requirements. It is the only law you need.

Until we choose to love, we must live with fear and restraint to protect ourselves from one another. But if we love our neighbor as much as we love ourselves, we will not want to harm or cheat him.

Without law there is anarchy. We have a choice to live under the law of fear and restraint or under the law of love and freedom.

When we are unloving we are harmful and destructive. Cruelty, hatred, violence, and injustice never can and never will be able to create.

You can self-righteously keep the law in every detail without loving, but you cannot truly love without keeping the law. If you really love, you will keep the law.

"If you love me, you will keep my commandments," Jesus said.

Don't deal with God legalistically. That's the way you deal with someone you fear.

To paraphrase Saint Augustine: "Love God with all your heart, and do as you please!"

You act in love even though it is not the safe thing to do. Love does not guarantee either success or survival in material terms.

You act in love even though it is not the "smart" thing to do. Love is seldom considered clever strategy or common sense.

*You act in love
because it is right.*

Antilove takes SOMETHING
and reduces it to nothing.
Love takes nothing
and makes it into SOMETHING!

Love Is Kind

*K*indness is the power that moves us to support and heal someone who offers us nothing in return. Kindness never says, "If that's the way he's going to treat me, see if I ever do anything nice for him again!" Kindness is kindness; it doesn't discriminate.

But kindness may not be love. Evil people can be charming. Nice is not synonymous with love. If I leave my manners behind when I come home from a party, I did not have real courtesy even there; I just pretended. Love is courteous, both privately and publicly.

You will often hear someone say, "I come home to relax. A person can't always be on his best behavior. If a man can't be himself in his own home, where can he? We can say anything to each other here. No one minds."

When there is this kind of inconsistency, we hear the expression, "You treat strangers better than me."

Love is not kind for its own convenience. Love is kind because it is kind. Kindness may receive its best test when we have been hurt. You cannot be truly kind to someone who has hurt you unless you have forgiven him. When you are kind you will not use the past against him. You will not bring up the hurt again, either to him or to anyone else. You will not allow your thoughts to dwell on the incident.

If you think of it in passing, you will immediately remember that it has been forgiven. When authentic forgiveness has taken place, your behavior will change. It must change.

Love is kind.

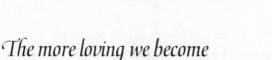

The more loving we become
      the more humble we become.
The more humble we become
      the more awed we are by the
      potential for abusing power.
Humble people are students—
      still asking questions.
Arrogant people have all the answers.
Humility is not pretentious.
Humility is simple.
Humility accepts itself for who it is—
      nothing more and
      nothing less.
Humility doesn't make announcements.
Humility is discovered. You just do the
loving thing, and maybe it will be found
out later.

Love Is Humble

*J*esus told the story about the Pharisees who blew trumpets to attract attention to their giving. And he warned the people, "Take care not to do your righteous deeds publicly to be admired, for then you will lose the reward from your Father in heaven."

*Humility makes no comparison
    because it is not competitive.
Pride is essentially competitive.
Pride wants to be richer
    or smarter
    or better-looking than anyone else—
to be above the rest.*

When competition is gone, pride is gone. Pride is a spiritual cancer that eliminates the very possibility of love or contentment or humility.

To speak of ourself as being less than others is false humility which is only pride in disguise.

True humility or unselfishness can have no tinge of self-pity, "martyrdom," or desire for either self-exaltation or condescension.

Whenever we find that our religious life is making us feel that we are good, or that we are better than someone else, we may be sure that we are not being acted upon by a God of love.

One of the greatest proofs that I am drawing upon the grace of God is that I can be humiliated without the slightest trace of anything but His grace.

Love Is a Decision

Love is an act of the will.
Love is a choice.
Love is a decision.
Love wills to act
in the other person's highest interest
regardless of how I feel.
Love is an act of obedience
to the commandment to love.
It is not an option.

If we earnestly desire to do God's will, we are obeying His commandment to
"Love God with all your heart,
And your neighbor as yourself."

Loving means you wish someone good whether you like him or not. Do not waste time wondering whether you really love your neighbor; just act as if you did. As soon as you do this, you will discover a great secret: When you are behaving as if you love someone, you will soon come to truly love him.

Do not try to manufacture good and right feelings. As C.S. Lewis suggests, "Ask yourself, 'If I were sure that I loved God, what would I do?' When you have found the answer, do it!"

> *Love is a decision of commitment.*
> *Love is a commitment forever,*
> > *a lifelong wager—*
> *not "as long as" or "until" anything.*
> *Love is a promise kept.*
> *Your love must be a permanent offer*
> *before I will give up*
> > *my masks*
> > *my roles*
> > *my games.*

> *If love were only a feeling, there would*
> *be no basis for the promise to love each*
> *other forever...*
> > *for better or worse,*
> > *for richer or poorer,*
> > *in sickness and in health.*

Feelings come and go, especially when things are for worse, for poorer, or in sickness.

nmitment frightens us because
possibilities. Every commit-
life: There is a birth and a

ever be again.
n never was.

on the line, and there is no
hat so many of us collapse.
s, we faint at the thought of
never returning.

It is the less-traveled road. It is the road of commitment.

Love
Is Just

*N*ever look for justice in this world—but never fail to give it!

If we would just practice this one thing, it would make an enormous difference in our relationships at all levels. But we have a difficult time reconciling love and justice, grace and judgment. How do we know the difference between justice and vengeance?

I can only understand and reconcile the relationship of love and the demand for justice and the need for forgiveness in light of God's reconciliation.

Justice demands judgment of wrongdoing. How can a God of justice allow anyone into heaven? What right do we have? On the one hand we have all fallen short of the requirements and on the other hand all of our goodness is "filthy rags" by comparison to the requirements.

Justice demands that we all be found guilty, but God in His infinite love has taken our place, absorbing the wrong and the pain. In our loving and humble acceptance of this substitution, we are set free.

If I am a loving person, my intent is to be just—to do what is right. Love will be just to my neighbor's
>reputation
>person
>property
>body.

Justice or injustice is primarily determined by *intention* of the people involved. No outward act or appearance can in itself be either just or unjust. We need to be careful in our demands for justice, lest we all receive what we deserve. We usually consider it unjust when we are stopped for speeding. We seldom consider it unjust when we are overlooked while speeding!

Jesus asked, "How can you say to your brother, 'Let me pull out the splinter in your eye,' when a beam is in your own eye?"

It is not my right to mete out justice, to decide guilt or innocence, to punish and to free. That responsibility belongs to the judge, both for society and ultimately to God.

When I or mine have been wronged, feelings are involved and become the determining factor. The result is revenge. Justice is *objective* — without feelings.

Justice is right conduct and treatment. It is fair and honest. The judgments of God are holy and right and free from any element of self-gratification or vindictiveness. Love never claims the right to cause anyone to suffer.

Love Overcomes and Transforms

Love transforms arrogance to humility,
    resentment to forgiveness,
    worry to trust,
    fear to courage,
    vindictiveness to mercy,
    strife to peace,
    inferiority to a sense of worth.

Real JOY is transformed sorrow.
Real PEACE is struggle and strife overcome.
Real FREEDOM is self-centeredness transformed into
    a passion for self-giving.

*E*vil in the world is to be overcome and transformed by love. Angels cannot share the joy that our salvation brings. Once I was blind, but now I see. I was lost but now am found.

In the book of Genesis the story is told of Joseph sold into slavery by his jealous brothers. At the time this seemed cruel and destructive. Many years later, after Joseph became the premier of Egypt, his brothers came seeking food. When Joseph recognized them and remembered what they did, he could have been arrogant, resentful, vindictive, and self-centered. Instead, he chose to let God's love transform him, and said, "You intended evil against me, but God meant it for good, to save the lives of many people."

Because of love, Joseph could be trusted to use his enormous power to serve the people.

Love Brings Balance

Love allows an acquaintance to become a friend.
Love keeps passion within the bonds of commitment.
Love keeps freedom from becoming license—
because love is responsible.
Love keeps security from becoming apathetic—
because love is active.
Love allows you to go for it—with good judgment.
Love gives boundless freedom—with order.
Love brings bonding without bondage—
Judgment blended with grace
Confrontation matched with caring
Truth spoken in love.

*W*ithout love, freedom is interpreted as "anything goes," and I become a slave to those things I call free expression.

Without love, security becomes a prison of rules and traditions to the loss of joy and spontaneity.

Love allows temperance without either indulgence or abstinence.

Every loving, conscientious parent is aware of this need for balance as he or she is faced with gratifying a child's instinctive demands of
    hunger
    bodily evacuation
    aggression
    sexual instincts
while at the same time keeping the child under discipline.

The parent must both restrain and liberate the child at the same time.

A parent teaches adventure with caution. He hopes to achieve boundless freedom with order.

Love brings balance.

Love Attracts Love

*E*very one of our relationships with another person is an expression of our real, individual life. If the expression of will does not call forth love, it isn't love.

If by means of an expression of life as a loving person you do not make yourself a loved person, then your love is impotent.

It is very easy to fool ourselves into believing that we are doing the loving thing when in reality there is a condition to our gift and the other person senses it.

If I don't like what I'm attracting, I need to look more deeply at what I am truly radiating.

True love is given with no thought of getting something back, but if it is indeed true love, somewhere and sometime love will probably be returned.

If you are unable to share a wise, outgoing love with other people, you have never received the redeeming, reconciling love that God has for you. "There will be no mercy for those who have shown no mercy. Mercy triumphs over judgment!"

Love cures.
It cures those who give it
and it cures those who receive it.

Love Is a Living Sacrifice

*L*ove is the power to willingly give myself sacrificially for another person. Love means the unreserved giving of myself for the benefit of the other, even if it costs me my life.

The ultimate value of love is not the personal power for happiness and fulfillment, but the power to willingly give myself for another person.

I must value my life to give sacrifice meaning. To take a risk or give up something I do not value has no virtue. Meaningful self-denial can only come from that which we esteem.

"Greater love has no man than that he give his life for a friend."

The greatest gift is the gift of myself. The true lover gives what is *alive* in himself. He gives of his
joy
interest
understanding
knowledge
humor
pain.

In giving of your life, you enrich the other person.

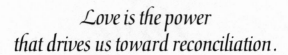

*Love is the power
that drives us toward reconciliation.*

*Love is not resentful
because it is forgiving.*

Love has no desire to control.

*Love has no need
to feel morally superior.*

Love lets the past die.

*Love moves people
to a new beginning.*

Reconciliation is love's ultimate goal.

Love Is Reconciling

*D*isobedience separated Adam from God and Adam from Eve. Being separated, they became strangers. As strangers they had not yet learned to love each other. This is made clear by the fact that Adam defended himself by blaming Eve rather than by trying to support her.

The deepest need of man is the need to overcome his separateness, to leave the prison of his aloneness. On a well-known stress test, the five highest-scoring stress factors had to do with separation:

death of spouse,

divorce,

marital separation,

jail term, and

death of a close family member.

The absolute failure to achieve reconciliation means insanity in a human sense. To be eternally separated is hell!

Only love can reconcile
and bring us to at-one-ment.

Love Is Not Obtained

*E*arly in life we began to perceive love as something for which we had to qualify. And the basic qualification was "goodness."

If you are "good" you will be loved.

If you are "bad" you will not be loved.

To be thought of as good, I must please the one I want to love me. And to please the one I want to love me I must meet his standards of goodness.

Our parents had standards. Our peers had standards. Our teachers had standards. Our teachers had standards. We had our own standards. And God has His standards.

We were very conscious of failing *all* of these standards at one time or another. We failed to measure up. We failed to qualify.

When we failed to measure up, we felt "bad." When we felt "bad" we did "bad" things that proved that they were right—that we really didn't deserve to be loved.

But love is not a matter of good and bad—it is a matter of life and death. To be loved is life. The better you love, the better you live. To truly be loved is to be loved in spite of our "badness" and even in spite of our "goodness."

We want to be rid of our faults,
    our feeling of nothingness.
We want to be justified.
We want to be redeemed.
We want love to tell us we are okay.
And God's love meets this need—
But, it is unearned—it is an act of grace.

Unless we understand and experience unconditional love, we are in a bind because we want to be loved for the wrong reasons. To be loved unconditionally, we can never again ask someone why he loves us.

Because unconditional love cannot be earned
I am set free
    from the insecurity of being loved
      when I am good
    and not being loved
      when I am bad.

Love is never on stage.
Love is not boastful, arrogant, or rude.
Boasting is a way of trying to look good
when I suspect I am not.
Only a lack of confidence has a need
for validation.
Arrogance is an anxious grasp for power
when I feel weak.
Rudeness is putting people down
in an effort to make myself look good.
Love has good manners in any society
at any level.
Love does what is appropriate.

Love Is Quiet Confidence

*W*hen you know you are loved you have hope.

When you have hope you have a quiet confidence in your future. With confidence you are able to stop struggling, to stop fighting other people for position and attention. Confidence has no need to dominate.

The quiet confidence that comes from hope sets us free to be concerned for the well-being of others.

Because we are confident and not threatened,
    we can give of
        our time
        our possessions
        our life
to others, with the quiet confidence that God will make it right. He who sees in secret rewards openly.

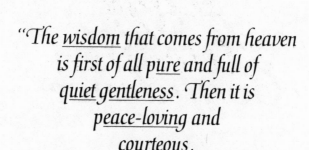

"The <u>wisdom</u> that comes from heaven is first of all p<u>ure</u> and full of quiet <u>gentleness</u>. Then it is p<u>eace-loving</u> and <u>courteous</u>. It <u>allows discussion</u> and is willing to <u>yield to others</u>. It is full of <u>mercy</u> and <u>good sense</u>. It is <u>wholehearted</u> and <u>straightforward</u> and <u>sincere</u>."

James 3:17

Love Pays Attention

Love listens.
Love communicates.
Love acknowledges and is sensitive
to the needs of the other person.
Love is aware.
Awareness means to open ourselves up
to the negative as well as the positive—
to grief, sorrow, and disppointment
as well as to joy and fulfillment.

To pay attention is to be responsible. The more responsible we are, the fewer people there are to blame.

Attention is a response. It is a voluntary act, not an obligation. In order to respond to the needs, expressed or unexpressed, of another human being, *I must be aware.* I will pay attention, and that usually means my *undivided* attention. I can't really listen to you while I am watching television.

If I love you, I will be constantly reading your needs, watching you with the look of love.

Are you discouraged and in need of my strength?

Are you lonely and need only my hand on yours?

Are you experiencing success and are inviting me to celebrate with you?

This kind of empathetic listening and looking is one of the deepest challenges of love.

When we feel heard, we feel valued, we feel loved. If you really believe that God loves you, you believe that He knows your name and that He is not too busy to listen to you. He will give you His undivided attention.

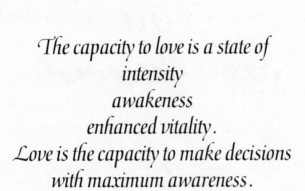

The capacity to love is a state of
intensity
awakeness
enhanced vitality.
Love is the capacity to make decisions
with maximum awareness.
Love pays attention.

Love Is Patient

*L*ove is not in a hurry. Love thinks long-range. It takes time to be a Good Samaritan.

Patience is a quality of constancy, of bearing up under trials, afflictions, persecutions, and discouragement with all joy!

"Is your life full of difficulties and testings? Then be happy, for when the way is rough, your patience has a chance to grow. So let it grow, and don't try to get out of your problems. For when your patience is finally in full bloom, then you will be ready for anything, strong in character, full and complete" (James 1:2-4 TLB).

Teaching a child patience is teaching him to love. He needs to learn patience with his parents' delays and denials, which is based on trusting their essential interest in his welfare. He also needs to learn patience with himself when he makes a mistake or fails in some way, trusting in his own ability to do better next time. He learns to turn his mistakes into learning experiences.

Here are a few ways a child can experience
patient love from his parents.

*He is allowed to make decisions
    and experience either the reward
    or the consequence.
He is made comfortable
    for a sense of security.
He is made uncomfortable at times
    to create change and growth.
He is understood,
    which means he is listened to.
He is encouraged to do his best,
    compared to no one's.
He is given undivided attention
    when it is needed.
He is forgiven for his faults,
    without reminders of the past.
He is allowed to grow up.*

Love Serves

*S*ervice is love's true nature. The role of servant is not bestowed or assumed, but chosen.

Leadership is bestowed upon a person who is by choice a servant *first*.

The only leadership deserving one's allegiance is that which is freely and knowingly granted by the led to the leader in response to and in proportion to the clearly evident *servant stature* of the leader.

People will freely respond only to individuals who are chosen as leaders because they are proven and trusted as servants.

When love serves, people grow.
While being served they become
> *healthier*
>
> *wiser*
>
> *freer*
>
> *more autonomous.*

The least privileged is benefited.
When love serves, the immature
> *the stumbling*
>
> *the inept*
>
> *the lazy*

are capable of great
> *dedication and heroism.*

Love causes a person to approach the position of leadership with awe rather than arrogance. There is no middle ground between arrogance and humility. One may not safely lead unless one is open and ready to receive the gifts of others.

A person or even a nation is perceived as arrogant when it is always in a positon of giving and seems to have no need of receiving anything from anyone.

We can only be truly loved in our poverty.

Love Is a Channel

Love is not a reservoir.
Love cannot be stored.
Love cannot be banked.
Love is an ebb and flow.
As I give love...I receive love.
Fear chokes the channel.
Love opens it up again.

*L*ove has a willingness to *receive* (even if not originally desired) as well as a willingness to let go again without grasping after repetition of the pleasure.

Love enjoys the moment; fear cannot. We are to love ourselves as God has loved us, not as an end in itself but as a means toward an end.

As we have freely received,
we freely give.

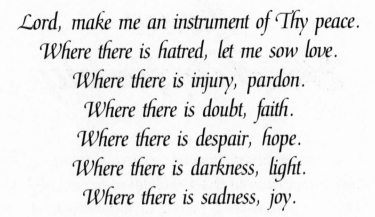

Lord, make me an instrument of Thy peace.
Where there is hatred, let me sow love.
Where there is injury, pardon.
Where there is doubt, faith.
Where there is despair, hope.
Where there is darkness, light.
Where there is sadness, joy.

O Divine Master, grant that I may not
so much seek to be consoled as to console,
To be understood as to understand,
To be loved as to love.

Saint Francis of Assisi

Love Is Forgiving

Love lets one begin again — without handicap.
Love forgives and forgets the failings of the one loved.
Forgiveness frees your "enemy" to change his mind.
Love makes it easy.
Vengeance makes it difficult.

When love forgives, it really wants the other person to be able to become better. If I want him to stay "bad" so I can justify my attitude, forgiveness has not taken place.

When I have really forgiven you, I don't ask God to punish you, even though He may.

Forgiveness is not about good people forgiving bad, or innocent people forgiving guilty people.

Forgiveness is about sinners forgiving sinners.

Jesus told a story about a palace servant who was forgiven for a large debt. His king forgave him a debt of 10,000 talents, a sum it would take 15 years to pay off in labor. After he was forgiven this enormous debt, the servant met a man who owed him a mere hundred denarii, a sum that could be worked off in a day. The king's servant demanded every cent to be paid. When the king heard this, he summoned the servant, took back his forgiveness, and threw him into prison to work off the talents that he owed.

The story is about God and us. If we act like the unforgiving servant, God will act like the king.

How often have we prayed, perhaps without understanding, "Forgive us our trespasses *in the same manner* that we forgive those who have trespassed against us."

Like every aspect of love, forgiveness is an act of the will; it is a choice. It is not accurate to say, "I *can't* forgive." It is more correct to say, "I *won't* forgive."

Forgiveness is a matter of the intention of the heart. Do you *want* to forgive? If you are *trying* to forgive — even if you forgive today and fail tomorrow, and forgive again the day after — you are making progress.

Love Is Costly

Love is indeed costly,
but its rewards make it worthwhile.

*E*verything in life has a price;
my only choice is which things I am willing to pay for.

In this life we cannot choose whether we suffer and die — only for what.

There is a price to pay for education.
There is a price to pay for ignorance.
There is a price to pay for attending
to good health.
There is a price to pay for
neglecting health.
There is a price to pay for attending
to relationships.
There is a price to pay for
neglecting relationships.
There is a price to pay for love.
There is a price to pay
for fear and hate.
We cannot choose whether we pay—
only for what!

John Powell in his book *Unconditional Love* put it this way:

"If you don't want to—
- break the fixation with self and give up your self-centeredness,
- learn how to care about and be sincerely dedicated to the satisfaction of another,
- become a sensitive listener, who hears what is said and some things that are not,
- postpone personal gratification to meet the needs of another,
- get in touch with your deepest feelings and most hidden thoughts,
- share your most vulnerable self as an act of love,

...if you don't want these things, then obviously you don't want love. If you prefer to be an island, a recluse, a narcissist, preferring to live in a world that has a population of one, love would rip out of your hands everything that you hold dear and clutch tightly."

Love Responds Creatively

The kingdom of God dwelling within us is best revealed in how we respond to being wronged.

Love responds creatively to wrong situations by overcoming with good.

In a loving relationship with God we are thankful in every situation because with God there are no second causes.

When we are complaining about—
    the way life has ill-treated us
    the undeserved frustration and trial we have met
    the way people have misunderstood and
        wronged us—
we feel we are justified in our resentful feelings.

But under no circumstance does love feel resentful or sorry for itself or react with bitterness or an unwillingness to forgive.

If it is my *intention* to love, it is not hypocritical to act as I earnestly desire to feel, even though the feelings may be very contrary at the moment.

When love responds creatively it becomes an act of worship. Worship removes myself from the center of attention and replaces self with the joyful awe of God. No longer can guilt and selfishness occupy the personal stage. No longer can emotional energies be sapped on miserable introspection.

Worship is the mental frame
of the mature and loving person.

In the Christlike mindset the immediate response to all human experience is a response of worship.

Whether that experience
is one of joy or sorrow,
it matters not.

Worship is the modus operandi
of the mature, loving, spiritual mind.

Love Is the Difference

*T*he question has been asked, "If you were arrested for being a Christian, would there be enough evidence to convict you?"

A better question might be, "What have you done this past week that only a child of God would do?" Some of the things that first come to mind, such as praying, worship, reading Scripture, or charity to the needy probably don't qualify, since most people in the world do some of these things at one time or another. For many people their religious rituals and traditions are nothing but a form of subculture.

I think we can find a clue to the answer in the words of Jesus: "It has been said that you should love your friends and hate your enemies, but I say to love your enemies!

Bless those who curse you,

Do good to those that hate you,

Pray for those who persecute you.

Only so can you be seen as children of your heavenly Father. If you love only those who love you, what good will it do? If you are friends only to those who are your friends, how are you different from anyone else? Even sinners do that."

This kind of loving doesn't make you a child of God, it *identifies* you as a child of God.

If the difference has something to do with our attitude toward our enemy, it is important to identify who our enemy might be.

An enemy is anyone we consider a threat — someone who could hurt or offend us, someone we feel justified to hate, someone we would like to put out of our life.

Your enemy could be someone who has lived close to you. It could be your husband, or an ex-wife, or a rebellious child, or an in-law, or a business partner.

Our natural inclination is to want to hate or hurt our enemy. The ultimate test of our relationship with the Father, that which identifies us as *His child*, may be when He asks, "What would you have me do to your enemy?"

The natural response is "Condemn him."

The child of God, the true lover, responds, "Bless him, and give me strength and courage to love him as You do."

To change our world, we will have to do it differently.

Love is the difference!

Love Is the Ultimate Success

Is the ultimate success to be:
>   the most beautiful person in the world?
>   the smartest?
>   the richest?
>   the most famous?
Or just to be loving?

*I*s it possible that the ultimate success of my life will not be judged by those who admire me for my accomplishments but by those who have seen their true beauty and worth in my eyes?

The ultimate achievement of "loving your neighbor" is the willingness to give your life for a friend. "Greater love has no man."

Love is an attitude toward *all* of God's creation, including myself. If it is right to love my neighbor as a human being, it must be a virtue to love myself also, since I am a human being too.

To love your neighbor as yourself implies that respect and love for your own integrity and uniqueness cannot be separated from respect and love and understanding for another person's individuality. Love for my own self is inseparably connected with love for every other person.

Love of others and love of self are not alternatives. An attitude of love toward ourselves will be found in all of us who are capable of loving others. We will indeed love others as we love ourselves. We will treat people as our equal.

Cancer patients were asked two questions. If you had but one hour to live:
> *Who would you spend it with?*
> *What would you remember?*
Their answer was:
> *People they loved.*
> *Good work that made a difference.*

In their last hour they did not recall their possessions, how much money they made, how powerful they were, or their fancy cars. They were truly aware of the Ultimate Success!

Love desires only the best for its object,
and the best is God!
The golden rule bids us give,
not what others <u>desire</u>,
but what they <u>need</u>.
The love which God's law requires
is love for the true God,
the God of holiness and wholeness.
Such love aims at the reproduction of God's holiness
in ourselves and in others.

Love Restores God's Image

In our journey toward moral,
      loving decision-making we —
First, love self for *our* own sake,
Then we love God for *our* sake.
Then we love God for *his own* sake, and
Finally, we love ourselves for God's sake.

*R*easonable self-love is a virtue wholly incompatible with what is commonly called selfishness.

Society suffers not from having too much of it but from having too little.

No unregenerate person can properly respect himself.

Self-respect belongs only to the person who lives in God and who has God's image restored to him.

True self-love is in turn conditioned by love to God as holy, and it seeks primarily not the *happiness* but the *holiness* (wholeness) of others.

Holiness is dedication to God as an internal controller and transformer of character.

Creation is one great unselfish thought—
the bringing into being creatures who can know
and experience the life that God knows.

To the spiritual person,
holiness and love are inseparable.

Love delivers us from selfishness.

Love restores God's image.

Love one another for God's sake!